The Standard Publishing Company, Cincinnati, Ohio.
A division of Standex International Corporation.
© 1992 by The Standard Publishing Company
All rights reserved.
Printed in the United States of America
99 98 97 96 95 94 93 92   5 4 3 2 1

Library of Congress Cataloging-in-Publication Data
Watson, Elaine.
Busy feet / Elaine Watson ; illustrated by Roberta K. Loman.
ISBN 0-78403-952-5
Library of Congress Catalog Card Number 91-46915

BUSY
FEET

Elaine Watson
illustrated by Roberta K. Loman

STANDARD
PUBLISHING

"He makes
my feet
like the feet
of a deer."

Psalm 18:33
New International
Version

God planned for feet.

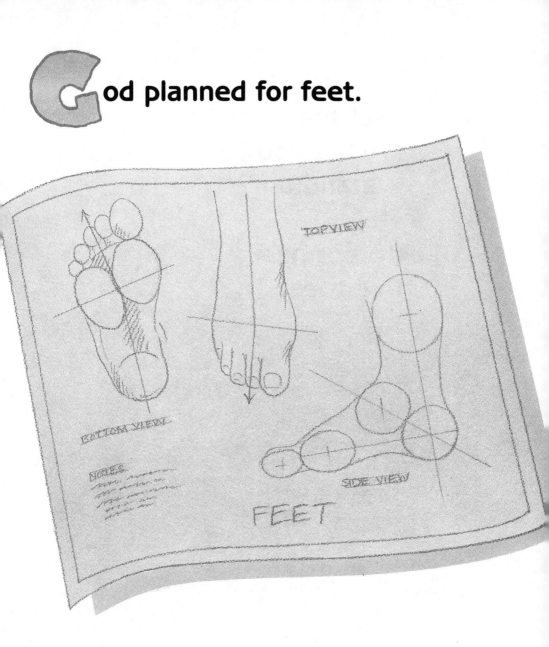

Feet are
what you
stand on.

Each foot has
five toes.

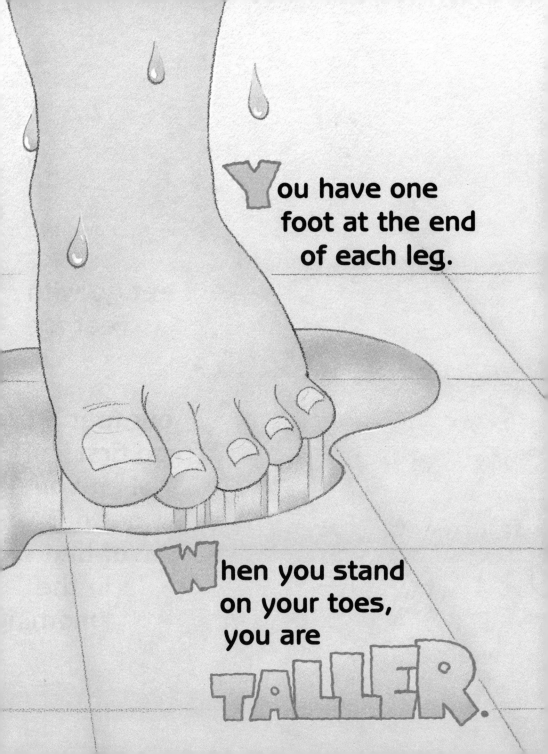

You have one
foot at the end
of each leg.

When you stand
on your toes,
you are
TALLER.

Feet go with
Feet are

Your feet
go first
when you
get out
of bed
in the
morning

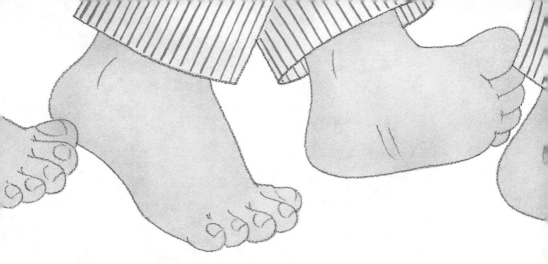

you everywhere.
very busy.

Feet walk
you to the
kitchen
to eat
breakfast.

Feet walk you
to a friend's house.

But feet can do more

They run with your dog.

than walk.   Feet **RUN!**

hey run to meet Mommy and Daddy coming home.

Feet climb
UP and DOWN.

Feet hop and jump.

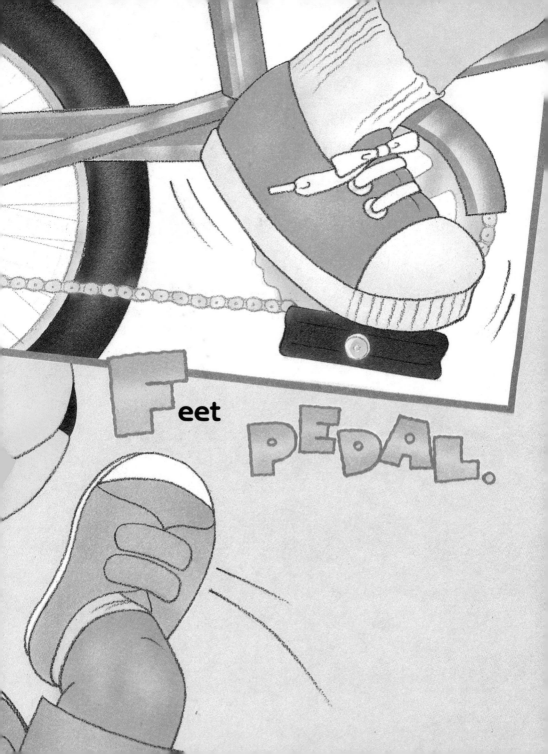

Feet PEDAL.

Feet wear shoes and socks

Feet wear slippers when you get ready for bed.

(most of the time).

n the summer, feet wear sandals.

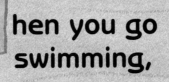hen you go
swimming,

and when you take a bath,
feet don't
wear anything.

Feet are ticklish.

At night your feet
are the last part of you
to get into bed.

Thank You, God,
for feet that

WALK, RUN, CLIMB, HOP, JUMP, KICK, and PEDAL.

Thank You
for my
busy feet!

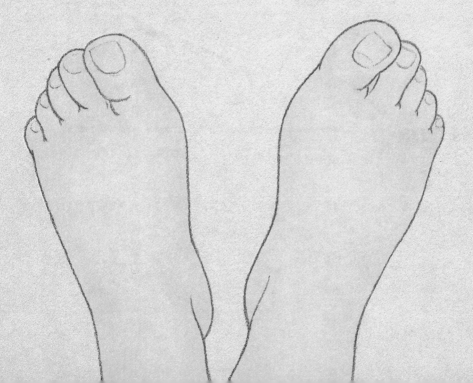